# AS THE INK BIDS SPLIT
Poetry Chapbook by Amelia Rose Averis

ISBN: 9798306029856

**Amelia Rose Averis 2025**
©™®
**Alien Buddha Press 2025**

### the ink birds

1. The things
2. One and each day you must wake up and chose
3. The last thing to do
4. Summer becomes this
5. Sleeping closeness
6. *Gretel in Darkness – Louise Glück*
7. the armchair
8. untitled *(i was to inherit the earth)*
9. New Year's Resolutions
10. The ache of the old mouth
11. toy house II
12. column advice: an is this
13. December
14. Golden girl you've been god awful
15. The moment you are not owed a thing
16. The Habits of Atoms

**The things**

Begin with the bed springs,
brass coffee pot, beads of the curtain sash

The dutiful revision of self
as artefact and certain light:

a child's wooden figures smoothed each time
by fondness
and desperate endeavour,
*move*, we say, *live again*

 the pink mountain, chess set, the coolness of tiles,
*please, my life , once more.* The gathered

more precious, more to place and kiss in line
you cannot take them with you, these beautiful things

        Even yourself you must leave here.

## One day and each day, you must wake and choose

On earth I cried for heaven,
Yet I came to heaven
and cried for earth.

Eventually realizing, they were not preceding but adjacent —
Reachable through what, not death
not birth,
— the watery mirror straddling each morning.

Remember when we walked closer to earth and examined each clover?
And now, you've surrendered, decided heaven is where you are not.

But turn your back to the sunsets, you can't: tell me why.
It is because love and wonder never leave us,
You can't help it        you will always run falling into fleeting
snow.

**The last thing to do**

The last week of November's
sharp mornings, the sun low
and blinding
You emerge from the house wincing
into white light like the end.

Cutting through tendrils of breath, showing air for what it is.
We move still amongst every word we ever said.

You fold and unfold the year on fraying edges,
breast pocket it and step outside,
the words peel like church bells sharpened,
The world is lit in beams that slice the coffee steam.

The year never ended; the world never stopped
The task of December: it was all decided already.
Emerge into what is — the white light like the end.

**Summer becomes this**

Try what you will, summer
becomes this: one evening in a field.
one sky and inward breath.

You will only spend one night
in the bed you slept in for a year, and some things will be stone certain
but mostly, everything you ever meant becomes the one final thing.

With the tunnel blinding, you will not remember
somewhere piano, laughter
But what song, what words

In memory we do things only once
The bike ride, the walk home,
Youth is one walk into one room,
and one walk out of it.

**sleeping closeness**

you sleep, murmuring
in oil painted strokes of chestnut.
those steady breaths brush my shoulder warm hazel
so tender,
like you've never known bad or how to be it.

You are harder and softer than anything I have ever known,
but here you will never go hungry.

I had a god once, now
he is this sleeping boy.

**Gretel in Darkness - Louise Glück**

*No one remembers. Even you, my brother,*

*summer afternoons you look at me though*
*you meant to leave,*
*as though it never happened.*

*we are there still and it is real, real,*
*that black forest and the fire in earnest*

*Gretel in Darkness, Louise Glück*

it's still there so I'm here,
the yellow room that floated on blue houses
where none of this has happened yet, no blood fire or clawing.

But I had to leave, brother.
it only became home when I did,
it's why I woke up on the doorstep again,
why when you looked at me I thought, I thought —

It's on fire now, friend, the room, the home,
the fire in earnest, and this is what is real

the assassin, still hopeful,
on fire in earnest.

**The armchair**

The afternoon drapery thinning gold
on amber bedsheets out to sea.
Honey-glass cools into night on the armrest
Revealing the hardened blue
evening sculpture
of where you sit to tie your shoes.

**untitled** *(I was to inherit the earth)*

I was not prepared for what I wanted but remembered what I came back for

I was to inherit the earth, all of its poems,

the life that dripped like warm honey onto paper,
I remember, remember the colour of
the beginning

I reach for the city that glows behind the hill,
the music in the next room like organs moving,

for laughter from the kitchen, sharp
rock salt,
someone humming.

**New Year's Resolutions**

Be kinder to my bones                                               1
and body                                                            2
with fresh fruit and charity,                                       3, 4
and to other bodies with letters                                    5
and holding.                                                        6
And to both, and the soft earth
with more time in the forest,                                       7
and time spent looking                                              8
at what I've not yet seen.


Incrementally and unimportantly become better                       9
at living, but
in truth the intangible is hard to measure, you barely notice —
    you do not know how kind you have become.

## The ache of the old mouth

Just before sleep, the watery dreams —
my feet are on the dashboard and also walking us somewhere
(probably ahead, why was I always ahead)
so much can be real.

                                                I say distorted things
                                   with my old mouth, gentle things

whilst my ghost eyes stay on the road:

                              the thank you that I believe sounds like
                                          I love you so much.

As I turn to look at you
I know I never turn
as it happened I never told you.

**toy house II**

That's us drinking the year at the kitchen table
in the purple light of youth and freedom
where I loved you so much, in that house
where we were kids together, who else can say that?
Who else knows that the same day always played from the beginning
and that the year was hours long?

**column advice: an is this**

stir,
rarely stay in one place for   long

always look back

have a strong attachment   to   longing.

feast On fragments of memory
and    a long-lost earth

whatever the          consequences
care deeply for a character who does
     unforgivable things

answer without
hesitation

stay faithful to this  amazing painful place

## December

december's glass anguish spine of
gratitude you are sure you must not have,
near shattered

suspended between the years of these days'

Teeth-sand. Sharp
'by this time', soft 'we'd just be-'
its shallow-deep and miles wideness,
it all still happening.

## Golden girl you've been god awful

I know it seemed like I robbed you cold and
came in your sleep and drove you out of your house.
*Yes Golden girl you've been god awful*
*You're the meanest person I've ever met.*
But i promise i didn't take anything i could keep,
my hands are empty, i also have no home,
*you've done away with the one good final thing*

                I know.

## The moment you are not owed a thing

How do I tell you how it felt
to cry
after choking on my eyes for so long
that my ribs had fused, I went days
without breathing
my throat clawed at air like a drowning
desperate mute
gulping silently at denial.

I landed and my ribs split winded
heaving everything up.
mortifying bleeding
confessions
of things I thought I owned, was owed.

Pulsing, bleeding, mocking things,
thrown up coughing
  on the (prayer) rug
the aborted aliens of human flesh begging
Where is the world I was promised?
Where's the oxygen? The beach?
Where are my legs?

**The Habits of Atoms**

The first thing: Eat a self-help book. Stare
at emptiness the way a dog barks at a doorway, obsess
over imagery of loss, only look
at yourself in candlelight.

Make poems either meaningful or interesting, feel
you should've always done the other, go home
 from the pub and meditate on ego death

get christmas from the loft in April, decide anger
is a sad child, wait
like furniture
and for the final unforgivable thing
wait for home to come to you like
a creature you have betrayed.

Walk the woods a retired greyhound,
look at your hands, watch
the showerhead, lift your diaphragm
with puppet strings,

This place will keep you alive.

## the sunset

1. But say it all came at once
2. Winter is a whale's eye
3. I think the boats became white witches
4. Mars had burnt itself blue
5. To where, I return
6. April Durrow, Offaly
7. The spring journals that are filled with summer
8. untiled II *(you loved everything because you were in pain)*
9. The quiet journey home
10. night lake
11. entire worlds
12. The dying lights look to the dying lights

## But say it all came at once

Darkening room like childhood sleep,
the days and decades
of rising bathwater creak restless, warming

haze moss pads your bones through, in June
you feel the flies land on each second
the winter pendulum echoes in stone hollow air.

But say it all came at once
blizzard of stars falling, biblical downpour
shattering the pavement
the sky has set the world on fire,

your miraculous self would turn up at the door, soaked
in a streetlamp halo saying:
'I'm kidnapping you get up      we're running,'

                                    You'd go in the middle of the night for it, abandon
*You could've gone on your own you know*
'We'll steal a van and scream naked into the sea,'
*rather than be kidnapped and bundled away*
'snow lasts a day but so does everything.'

## Winter is a whale's eye

The October sunset bruises the horizon - guttural sobs
of navy and purple rest on the sea, the tender heaviness
of colours bleeding from the inside.

That whale song of winter starts up again, everything swallows itself,
I make a home in its stomach.

**I think the boats become white witches**

The harbour screams from inside itself,
the masts wail worship -- yet in stillness
and the ropes, sermons hum stories

in the voices ricocheting off steadfast boats
swaying together,
each with a light, like vigil candles in cupped hands.

The wind grips the masts bent double, braces
inhales and screams again.

A choir of these, crescendoing, scream with it
out to sea where things aren't tied in place.
but here, this,
invisible violence.

## Mars had burnt itself blue

mars had burnt itself blue,
and the fog, my word
it was endless what we couldn't see:
That everything good was here on earth,
we just had to believe it.
The two lovers walking became one figure on the bigger beach
that was underwater this morning but unfurled for them
when they woke to find more land to walk

## To where, I return

I didn't come back for a long time
when I did the matchbox was damp
and the moon where it belly laughed, screamed
a flint of marble
in a still mirage.

I upturned rocks at low tide — the world a wet desert, looking
for the soft light of conversation
that must have been buried in the harbour.

There I saw
as the ink birds split the sunset
the edges of the indistinct begin again
to shimmer

and I wrote — *it is all retrievable by nature.*

## April Durrow, Offaly

you cannot make up that much green
that april, the vast dryness.
when every sound was creaking wood.

nothing absorbed anything, the moss kindled
the lane like a metal drum,  the bike echoed.
Skin burnt late into the evening, forearms, the smell of singeing.

The dog and I watched the fields, inside in turn for water, cold tiles.
The crescendo of flies in the silence
between the distant machinery cutting
        the distant grass.

## The spring journals that are filled with summer

It's the first of May and then the fifth,
you lie in the sun and a week passes and half the year, all day
is mid afternoon, summer becomes.

a warm world and you will be called daily for your scene.
June will fling the doors open and tell you to run and you will.

*It will all be beautiful, the beach will unfurl. The tide won't come in until you do,* spring says.

There is an evening you will not notice the temperature
the warm water air will never turn black, the same day will play over in shades of blue and smirk
at the idea of things ending.

Hairs bleach, skin stains. We are the photograph
negative, remembering
how it feels to be in these bodies holding
a cold bottle neck in a warm hand, my palm singeing on your driftwood back.

We are lighter
for less clothes so it is easier to touch and to move, we can be children
in the grass rusting and sweetening,
in the way the earth smells like memory, less like earth

weathered men talk in the fields
of summer or something else
*'it won't be before its time'* they say
perhaps everything.

**untitled II** (*you loved everything because you were in pain*)

I found you, flightless bird
ivy tethered to the graves

the stone doesn't warm this late in the year,
but something sits me and stays me
and says: draw. feel.
you are in pain, so love everything

## The quiet journey home

Everyone is the only one left
                           on earth: the moon is full
the audience gone
and behind this alien curtain velvet,
things begin again and resume.

Poets and dancers come alive from these bodies
               these dog-tired men.

**night lake**

The streetlamps lined in mourning, heads bowed like widows
in falling veils of mist and light

they are learning that night is not time,
but place to be inside of, held by or under

as the world fills as a lake, over houses
buoyant with manmade day, steadfast against tide.

In grey and blue the gorse crests,
the walls swell, hills break,

white shapes float on the water
smaller shapes sink in receding.

Behind the hill the day's embers burning
the final glow, a tiring effort

Someone stokes evening coal
Please, one longer day

**entire worlds**

Let me show you something specific.
This time of night
the fish, the people, their glass houses,
the chairs float in empty offices.
Tell me the town is not an aquarium,
the towering glass fish tasks, glowing from within,
the restaurant
a silent film in yellow light

they can't see us but watch: entire worlds within a world.

**The dying lights look to the dying lights**

The smell of soap and night,
at the bathroom's open window
where the stars
will fall tomorrow into blinding frost
from the clearness, freezing
only half of everything
we wanted
freezing
between the dying light and us
burning rage against it.

Amelia is an English literature graduate and journalist, but her best work can be found in her nine years of journals – the organs of her poems.

Printed in Great Britain
by Amazon